Piano Concerto
No. 20, K466
&
Piano Concerto
No. 21, K467

Wolfgang Amadeus Mozart

DOVER PUBLICATIONS, INC.
Mineola, New York

Published in Canada by General Publishing Company, Ltd., 30 Lesmill Road, Don Mills, Toronto, Ontario.

Bibliographical Note

This Dover edition, first published in 1999, is a republication of two works in "Serie 16: Concerte für das Pianoforte" of *Wolfgang Amadeus Mozart's Werke. Kritisch durchgesehene Gesammtausgabe,* originally published by Breitkopf & Härtel, Leipzig, 1877–9. Newly added are lists of contents and instrumentation, as well as the excerpt from the 1956 article on Mozart by Aaron Copland.

International Standard Book Number: 0-486-40868-X

Manufactured in the United States of America
Dover Publications, Inc., 31 East 2nd Street, Mineola, N.Y. 11501

CONTENTS

I like Mozart best when I have the sensation I am watching him think . . . [His] pellucid thinking has a kind of sensitized objectivity all its own: one takes delight in watching him carefully choose orchestral timbres or in following the melodic line as it takes flight from the end of his pen . . . It is the happy balance between flight and control, between sensibility and self-discipline, simplicity and sophistication of style that is his particular province . . . [He has] tapped once again the source from which all music flows, expressing himself with a spontaneity and refinement and breathtaking rightness that has never since been duplicated.

Aaron Copland

From his article for *High Fidelity*
January 1956

Piano Concerto No. 20
in D Minor, K466

(February 1785)

INSTRUMENTATION

2 Flutes [Flauti, Fl.]
2 Oboes [Oboi, Ob.]
2 Bassoons [Fagotti, Fag.]

2 Horns in D, B♭("B") [Corni, Cor.]
2 Trumpets in D [Trombe, Trbe.]

Timpani

Piano Solo [Pianoforte]

Violins I, II [Violino]
Violas [Viola]
Cellos & Basses [Violoncelli, Vcl. / Bassi]

Piano Concerto No. 20

I.

II. Romanze

154

III. Rondo

Allegro assai.

Flauto.
Oboi.
Fagotti.
Corni in D.
Trombe in D.
Timpani in D.A.

Pianoforte.

Violino I.
Violino II.
Viola.
Violoncello e Basso.

Allegro assai.

41

Piano Concerto No. 21
in C Major, K467

(March 1785)

INSTRUMENTATION

2 Flutes [Flauti, Fl.]
2 Oboes [Oboi, Ob.]
2 Bassoons [Fagotti, Fag.]

2 Horns in C, F [Corni, Cor.]
2 Trumpets in C [Trombe, Trbe.]

Timpani

Piano Solo [Pianoforte]

Violins I, II [Violino]
Violas [Viola]
Cellos & Basses [Violoncelli, Vcl. / Bassi]

Piano Concerto No. 21

I.

91

74

78

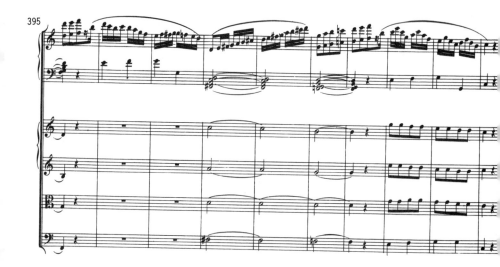

END OF EDITION

DOVER FULL-SIZE ORCHESTRAL SCORES

THE SIX BRANDENBURG CONCERTOS AND THE FOUR ORCHES-TRAL SUITES IN FULL SCORE, Johann Sebastian Bach. Complete standard Bach-Gesellschaft editions in large, clear format. Study score. 273pp. 9 x 12.
23376-6 Pa. **$12.95**

COMPLETE CONCERTI FOR SOLO KEYBOARD AND ORCHESTRA IN FULL SCORE, Johann Sebastian Bach. Bach's seven complete concerti for solo keyboard and orchestra in full score from the authoritative Bach-Gesellschaft edition. 206pp. 9 x 12.
24929-8 Pa. **$11.95**

THE THREE VIOLIN CONCERTI IN FULL SCORE, Johann Sebastian Bach. concerto in A Minor, BWV 1041; Concerto in E Major, BWV 1042; and Concerto for Two Violins in D Minor, BWV 1043. Bach-Gesellschaft edition. 64pp. 9⅜ x 12¼.
25124-1 Pa. **$6.95**

GREAT ORGAN CONCERTI, OPP. 4 & 7, IN FULL SCORE, George Frideric Handel. 12 organ concerti composed by great Baroque master are reproduced in full score from the *Deutsche Handelgesell-schaft* edition. 138pp. 9⅜ x 12¼.
24462-8 Pa. **$12.95**

COMPLETE CONCERTI GROSSI IN FULL SCORE, George Frideric Handel. Monumental Opus 6 Concerti Grossi, Opus 3 and "Alexander's Feast" Concerti Grossi—19 in all—reproduced from most authoritative edition. 258pp. 9⅜ x 12¼.
24187-4 Pa. **$13.95**

LATER SYMPHONIES, Wolfgang A. Mozart. Full orchestral scores to last symphonies (Nos. 35–41) reproduced from definitive Breitkopf & Härtel Complete Works edition. Study score. 285pp. 9 x 12.
23052-X Pa. **$14.95**

PIANO CONCERTOS NOS. 17–22, Wolfgang Amadeus Mozart. Six complete piano concertos in full score, with Mozart's own cadenzas for Nos. 17–19. Breitkopf & Härtel edition. Study score. 370pp. 9⅜ x 12¼.
23599-8 Pa. **$16.95**

PIANO CONCERTOS NOS. 23–27, Wolfgang Amadeus Mozart. Mozart's last five piano concertos in full score, plus cadenzas for Nos. 23 and 27, and the Concert Rondo in D Major, K.382. Breitkopf & Härtel edition. Study score. 310pp. 9⅜ x 12¼.
23600-5 Pa. **$16.95**

GREAT ROMANTIC VIOLIN CONCERTI IN FULL SCORE, Ludwig van Beethoven, Felix Mendelssohn and Peter Ilyitch Tchaikovsky. The Beethoven Op. 61, Mendelssohn, Op. 64 and Tchaikovsky, Op. 35 concertos reprinted from the Breitkopf & Härtel editions. 224pp. 9 x 12. 24989-1 Pa. **$12.95**

MAJOR ORCHESTRAL WORKS IN FULL SCORE, Felix Mendelssohn. Generally considered to be Mendelssohn's finest orchestral works, here in one volume are: the complete *Midsummer Night's Dream; Hebrides Overture; Calm Sea and Prosperous Voyage Overture;* Symphony No. 3 in A ("Scottish"); and Symphony No. 4 in A ("Italian"). Breitkopf & Härtel edition. Study score. 406pp. 9 x 12. 23184-4 Pa. **$19.95**

COMPLETE SYMPHONIES, Johannes Brahms. Full orchestral scores. No. 1 in C Minor, Op. 68; No. 2 in D Major, Op. 73; No. 3 in F Major, Op. 90; and No. 4 in E Minor, Op. 98. Reproduced from definitive Vienna Gesellschaft der Musikfreunde edition. Study score. 344pp. 9 x 12. 23053-8 Pa. **$15.95**

THE VIOLIN CONCERTI AND THE SINFONIA CONCERTANTE, K.364, IN FULL SCORE, Wolfgang Amadeus Mozart. All five violin concerti and famed double concerto reproduced from authoritative Breitkopf & Härtel Complete Works Edition. 208pp. 9⅜ x 12¼. 25169-1 Pa. **$12.95**

17 DIVERTIMENTI FOR VARIOUS INSTRUMENTS, Wolfgang A. Mozart. Sparkling pieces of great vitality and brilliance from 1771–1779; consecutively numbered from 1 to 17. Reproduced from definitive Breitkopf & Härtel Complete Works edition. Study score. 241pp. 9⅜ x 12¼. 23862-8 Pa. **$13.95**

WATER MUSIC AND MUSIC FOR THE ROYAL FIREWORKS IN FULL SCORE, George Frideric Handel. Full scores of two of the most popular Baroque orchestral works performed today—reprinted from definitive Deutsche Handelgesellschaft edition. Total of 96pp. 8¼ x 11. 25070-9 Pa. **$8.95**

FOURTH, FIFTH AND SIXTH SYMPHONIES IN FULL SCORE, Peter Ilyitch Tchaikovsky. Complete orchestral scores of Symphony No. 4 in F minor, Op. 36; Symphony No. 5 in E minor, Op. 64; Symphony No. 6 in B minor, "Pathetique," Op. 74. Study score. Breitkopf & Härtel editions. 480pp. 9⅜ x 12¼. 23861-X Pa. **$22.95**

ROMEO AND JULIET OVERTURE AND CAPRICCIO ITALIEN IN FULL SCORE, Peter Ilyitch Tchaikovsky. Two of Russian master's most popular compositions in high quality, inexpensive reproduction. From authoritative Russian edition. 208pp. 8⅜ x 11¼. 25217-5 Pa. **$10.95**